The Wit and Wisdom of
Penguins & Puffins

This is a STAR FIRE book

STAR FIRE BOOKS
Crabtree Hall, Crabtree Lane
Fulham, London SW6 6TY
United Kingdom

www.star-fire.co.uk

First published 2008

08 10 12 11 09

1 3 5 7 9 10 8 6 4 2

Star Fire is part of The Foundry Creative Media Company Limited

The CIP record for this book is available from the British Library.

ISBN: 978 1 84786 215 0

Printed in China

Thanks to: Chelsea Edwards and Nick Wells

Images courtesy of Fotolia: page 22 © Gail Johnson; 61 © Ian Thompson.

Images courtesy of iStockphoto: pages 4, 66 © Andrew Howe; 42 © Marco Kopp; 59 © doubleus;
63 © Lorenzo Codacci; 65 © Paul Tessier.

Images courtesy of Shutterstock: pages 1, 3, 29, 40, 48 © Steve Estvanik; 7 © Jeff Goldman;
9 © Maxim S. Pometun; 10 © Noah Strycker; 13, 16, 45 © Grigory Kubatyan; 14, 24, 68 © Armin
Rose; 19 © Marco Rametta; 20 © Henk Bentlage; 27 © Xavier Gallego Morell; 30 © Jose Alberto
Tejo; 32, 37 © Jeff Goldman; 34 © Tom Cummins; 39, 72 © Galina Barskaya; 47 © David Garry;
51 © Kitti; 52 © Gail Johnson; 54 © Creasence; 57 © ecoventurestravel; 71 © Eric Gevaert.

The Wit and Wisdom of
Penguins & Puffins

Ulysses Brave

Foreword

As you may know I have spent many years studying the habitats and habits of the animals of the world. I have always felt that such observation is useful in understanding the behaviour of the presumed-superior homo sapiens. Penguins and puffins have a special place in my study because they are such gentle, forgiving creatures, whose wisdom reaches beyond their subtle behaviour and carefully calibrated mannerisms.

Ulysses Brave

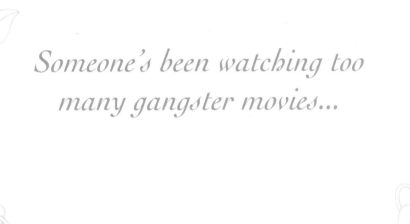

Someone's been watching too many gangster movies...

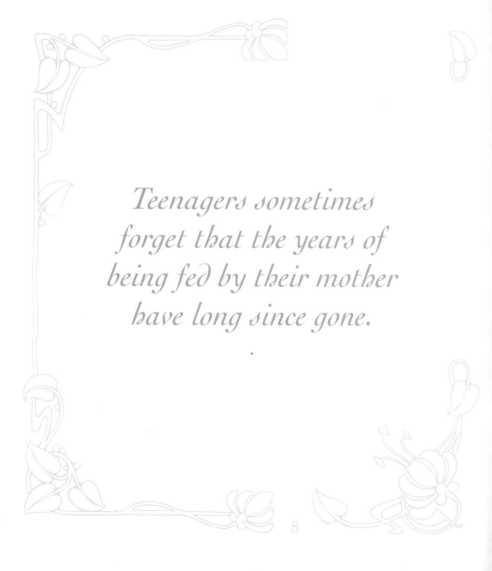

*Teenagers sometimes
forget that the years of
being fed by their mother
have long since gone.*

Try to look fierce when playing the Four Horsemen of the Apocalypse!

Always look both ways
before crossing the iceflows.

When leaping ahead,
make sure there is a
safe landing in front.

If you reach a dead-end in your life, don't just accept it, go back the way you came!

'So, we're lost then?'

If you have eaten a particularly lumpy piece of food, you may need to swim around a little to work it off.

Try not to eat all of the
shopping on your way home...

23

If your back muscles fail you,
take some specialist advice.

Careful self-assessment can alert you to the need for a bath and therefore reduce potential social embarrassment.

Even penguins suffer from furballs.

*It's so much fun
going down, but wait
until they have to go home!*

Be careful of infectious
foot diseases at the local
swimming baths.

'Not thinking of
jumping are you?'

If you're having an affair,
be careful about touching in
public. Standing too close
together is such a giveaway.
So is standing too far apart.

'Get off mum, my friends
are looking!'

Let the little ones in first – they can test the temperature of the water!

There are often subtle differences between twins. One of these is male.

Five minutes of pilates every day will improve your core strength.

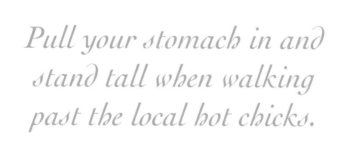

Pull your stomach in and stand tall when walking past the local hot chicks.

*Don't try your secret agent moves
when everyone is in a hurry.*

Always check to see if the sky is about to fall.

Don't let flying vegetation disturb your group meditations.

*Living simultaneously
in parallel worlds can give
you a headache.*

*Living life on the edge
won't suit everyone!*

In a carefully structured society it can be lonely at the top, although the views are fantastic.

If walking on water fails,
try flying and walking at
the same time...

When performing your famous love-display, make sure that the object of your desire is actually paying attention.

Try to ensure that your landing pad is free of all obstruction.

'Haven't I seen you somewhere before?'

Sometimes it can be worth practising swimming at home.

Some might consider
french-kissing on a first
date to be a little
too forward.

See you again...